... A N D

God

Stepped In

*My Journey through Healing
a Traumatic Brain Injury*

Candace Booth ND, PhD, OSL

NEWMAN SPRINGS PUBLISHING
320 Broad Street
Red Bank, NJ 07701

First originally published by Newman Springs Publishing 2022

ISBN 978-1-68498-629-3 (Paperback)
ISBN 978-1-68498-630-9 (Digital)

Printed in the United States of America

Contents

When I rescued my dog, Daisy Mae, I realized
I had a lot of undoing with her before she was
able to learn new things to help her feel safe and happy.

This is what this book is about for me.

Candace

Acknowledgments

Although this is a short book, it was born because of others who stepped in to walk my healing path mentally, emotionally, physically, and spiritually with me. Without their input and support, neither I nor this short memoir would have made it into print. I am blessed to know them.

I would like to thank the following:

Father Mark Lafler, priest and great teacher of the classes I attend at the Episcopal Church. He has been such a great inspiration for me on my journey to healing and becoming a devout Christian as well as a student of the Bible. He graciously accepted my request to write the back cover.

Deacon Kim Spear played a huge role in inspiring me to become a member of the Order of Saint Luke healing ministry. She helped me awaken to the powerful healing lessons of Jesus and understand the importance of healing prayer.

Deacon Bob and his lovely wife, Karin, who not only read through the book but offered valued feedback and encouragement to help hone my lack of knowledge as new student of Christianity.

My great friend and biblical teacher Marsha Hueratis for the many hours we spent in discussion about the Scriptures that support my healing experience throughout the book. Her knowledge and patience were sorely needed.

My son, Max Wettstein, who believed in my potential to heal my traumatic brain injury without truly knowing if I could. His dogged determination helped me push harder to never give up. He also helped me realize it was important to write my experience down especially for others who are suffering with similar healing challenges.

Introduction

by Max Wettstein

It was 9:00 p.m. when my phone rang, and I was informed that my mother was barely conscious and being loaded aboard an emergency helicopter flight to be transported from the rehabilitation center she was staying, in order to recover from her recent hip replacement and broken femur because of complications, to a specialty hospital to try and save her life with emergency surgery for a possible traumatic brain injury (TBI). I was in California, and she was in Florida. I knew I had to get there as quickly as possible. I put the phone on speaker so my wife could make plane reservations while I continued to gather more information about what happened to my mother and her escalating condition. We basically declared a family emergency and dropped everything so I could leave on the earliest flight in the morning.

What I was piecing together from the phone call and the background I already knew up to that moment seemed an unlikely and unimaginable combination of mishaps and mistakes, culminating in this final catastrophic traumatic brain injury—an insidious event that went totally unnoticed by the professionals in charge of my mother's care. These people were delinquent in their duties. (None of whom were ever held accountable much less empathetic.) Those critical first minutes and hours immediately after my mother lost her balance in the bathroom, causing her to fall backward and hit her head on a steel railing in the shower and subsequently slam her head on the tile floor where she lay helpless and screaming for help, could have meant the difference in lessening the ensuing damage she suffered, if only the professional in charge of her care had done their job and followed any kind of concussion protocol. But since there was no blood or laceration, two nurses carried my mother back to her bed, gave her more pain medication, and told her not to move again without permission. Then they shut and door and left her to "sleep off the headache." This is not how to treat someone who had a possible concussion.

Her headache did not go away. It got worse very quickly. Hours later, by the time her caregivers decided to check on her again, my mother was incoherent and nearly unresponsive. She was dizzy and vomiting. Those in charge of the rehab facility finally took the situation seriously and began taking emergency steps. It was almost too late because nobody knew my mother's brain was bleeding internally from striking her head and being on blood-thinning medication as prescribed by the surgeon who did her hip and leg surgery, which ultimately caused a blood clot to form in her lung.

My mother's condition was deteriorating quickly while the helicopter was en route to the hospital where a brain surgeon who specialized in brain bleeds made preparations for surgery. She was officially diagnosed with subdural hematoma: a buildup of blood on the surface of the brain, creating pressure, and this pressure was rapidly causing brain damage and threatening her life.

As I tried to sleep for a bit that night, we did not know if my mother was going to live through the night. When I awoke and was headed to the airport, she was still in surgery. By the time my flight departed, her surgery was over. The surgeon told us, "She will live, but at this point, we have no idea what function her brain will have." This was good news, but equally alarming. In these situations, with loved ones, everybody reacts and handles things differently. There are lots of emotions, even more questions and pondering of past mistakes that if anyone of the people involved had reacted sooner, this terrible disaster might not have happened. There is a lot of second-guessing and some blaming. For me, I immediately felt guilty for not living closer to her, for not doing more and being a better son. I felt a bit helpless. Yes, I was on the first flight out to see her, but what exactly could I do to help her situation? Would she even know I was there?

When I arrived at the hospital and at her bedside, the one thing I did not do was panic. The first sight of her was devastating. In this case, not panicking with knee-jerk reactions seemed to help even though it literally meant I was almost doing nothing except be present. The burning fire was out because she was out of surgery and stable. I had time to take a deep breath as she remained in care in the ICU for several days. I am a pilot, and throughout many years of emergency training, there is no instance for panic. Urgency, yes; but panic, never. Remain calm.

The other thing I've learned to do during *ground zero* or any kind of crisis is to play a mind game with myself known as *worst-case scenario*. This sounds basic, and in a time of crisis, it can be a good coping mechanism once the *raging fire* is put out. It helps my process to immediately bottom-line something and distill it down to my biggest fear, face it head on, and come up with a rough solution to quickly see the light at the end of the tunnel. It helps me reframe a crisis to another challenge and gain resilience. Then hopefully, the situation would get resolved in a better way when compared with the initial absolute worst case. To be candid, in this case, my worst fear was that my mother would be totally mentally incapacitated, would need full-time hospital type care, or at the very least, a live-in nurse to assist in her most basic needs. The worst would truly be that I would have lost my mother as I knew her and would not be able to afford proper long-term care.

It turns out that no panicking or making any reactionary or rash decisions about my mother's recovery (to the point of some people thinking I was in denial or even lazy) was the best strategy for her very long road to recovery. The thing about recovering from a TBI is, it can take a long time to make rational decisions and measure the progress of the person. Looking back, it almost felt like many of the decisions regarding the proper next step in her recovery became obvious and timely. It was all new territory for me, other than having a close friend who had recovered from a TBI as well and watching what his wife, a cardiac intensive care nurse, go through. However, she had some concussion protocol training. I had also watched some documentaries on extreme athletes who suffered severe head trauma.

My mother and I embarked on a journey together. In the beginning, it was incoherent and almost void of any conversation during phone calls (three times per day) while helping her focus on learning how to walk again. After a few more falls and balance issues, the nurses and therapists ordered her to remain in a wheelchair at all times (and she was still trying to recover from a broken leg and hip replacement surgery). At one point, my mother lost all confidence to attempt walking again from the negative feedback she was receiving from those who should have been offering motivation and support as she drifted in and out of consciousness. Reclaiming the most basic lifestyle tasks would be next. In the beginning, it did not look very promising. It seemed like she needed a miracle. I never gave up believing she had a chance to recover. Even her three neurologists had no idea if she would fully recover or what functions she would regain. We took it day by day. Many friends, family, and previous work colleagues prayed for her healing. Some seemed like angels.

The many rehab and assisted-living facilities my mother moved in and out of were sketchy at best, and very expensive. In hindsight, she and I realized the importance of having a next-of-kin advocating for you. She was often labeled *noncompliant*, when in fact, she didn't have enough brain function to understand what was happening, and she was often terrified. She also needed someone to tell her story from start to finish when another doctor or therapist was introduced into her care team—to keep them all on the same page. There was treatment confusion and even a chance of harm—like seventeen different prescriptions all at once by different doctors who did not consult with one another. The side effects were having a negative impact, since initially my mother was almost incoherent and had little to no short-term memory. Ironically because of this, she can't remember most of the trauma pain, neglect, and loneliness she experienced during her stay in assisted living. I'll never forget once when I flew in to visit her and check her progress, the bed she slept in was full of her urine, and she didn't even realize it. I changed the sheets myself. There was no use in holding anyone accountable in these places.

What you are about to experience in reading this book is my mother's story, in her own words, of her three-year road to recovery and her self-commitment to becoming well. You can decide for yourself if her complete healing is a miracle—from a combination of three catastrophic injuries to having no seizures, teaching classes, driving and living fully independent again. It's a quick read with no wasted words.

One can argue that the brain is already a perfect creation, nothing short of miraculous. But a damaged brain that is remapped and rewired into almost a new and more enlightened person—now that is intriguing.

Max

PART I

Inspiration

Just So You Know

Initially, there was no way for me to know how sick I was because my brain was becoming a new and different brain. I could only focus on the present moment. I didn't remember the past and had no clue there was a future. Daily, I was challenged to find a *new normal* and deal with the leftover trauma that a TBI (traumatic brain injury) causes (physically, mentally, and emotionally). Five months elapsed from the time of my initial injury, during which I was housed in four different rehab facilities before I was able to go home. Insurance was the primary factor for all the moves. The policy I had only allowed a six-week stay, and then it was time to move on.

I didn't make much progress at the first two rehab centers because I was suffering constant brain seizures and paralysis on the left side of my body and was in a wheelchair. I was medicated to help control the pain and various other issues the medical world deemed necessary.

When I was in rehab 3, I was still suffering from pain and paralysis; however, there was a determined physical therapist who took me under her wing. She was dedicated to helping me stand holding onto double bars until I could finally take a few steps with a walker with two people assisting me. It required a lot of motivation on her part because I didn't have any stamina and was afraid. She didn't tolerate any whining on my part. By the time I moved to rehab 4 with the help of two other people, I could shuffle walk up and down a long hall with my walker. The pain was still very intense. TBI brain exercises were finally added to my healing program to help me regain neurological function, assist with my erratic behavior, ease my frustration, and rebuild my communication skills.

By the time I was relocated to rehab 4, I was finally able to put the wheelchair away and use a walker on my own. My brother bought me a rolling walker with a seat, which made life easier. My self-motivation and self-awareness started waking up. Gradually, my new memory reminded me I knew about herbal medicine and natural healing remedies, so I could begin to wean myself off the prescriptions, which were creating a host of negative side effects. I was beginning to feel some control over my life.

I was told by the medical people in charge of me I could not go home until I could go the bathroom alone, dress myself, and walk unassisted. I mastered those challenges in six weeks albeit…far from perfect. I kept a cane handy just in case. I still did not remember how to use my computer, but I was able to go home…with no home health care (insurance). I was fortunate to have friends who helped me with food and driving. Most of all, I still had my son, Max, and wonderful wife, Donna, looking out for me. Though they lived three thousand miles away, they called me daily sometimes (two to three times) and flew in a couple of times to offer love and support to inspire me until I could relearn now to inspire myself. This became easier. Without knowing why and because my awareness still had a gaping hole, another power was fully involved in healing *my mind, body, and spirit*, because God had stepped in.

I had yet to realize He had been there all along.

The Miracle

Over the next several weeks, several amazing things slowly began to happen. They aren't all in a specific order as many of them overlap because of people and events that simultaneously came into my life.

Little did I know that PTSD (post-traumatic stress disorder) was going to challenge my healing progress. Odd little fears would affect me often. It was interesting and sad to discover who remained in my friend circle and who didn't. I didn't know why. As time went by, it didn't really matter because as I grew and changed and began to build new relationships with some outstanding people.

Many in my neurology world were surprised that my brain healed from the subdural hematoma, including my surgeon. When I took a trip to UF Shands Neurological Hospital to see him and thank him, he told me I was doing awesome! And *Healthy Living Magazine* wrote a story about me entitled "Mindblown" because I wasn't supposed to live, much less get a functioning brain back.

It took me a few months to wean myself from all the medications and build a program of healthy foods and natural supplements to feed my brain as well as exercises to boost dendrites and neurons. I also had great support from my primary care dude, Dr. Milton Arana, and my great eye doctor, Dr. Jeffrey Sheridan. I had to drop two neurologists along the way who couldn't get past the point that I would always have brain seizures…even after my last EEG in August of 2018 showed my brain was electrically sound.

As 2018 rolled to an end, I was slowly able to get my confidence and work mojo back and start teaching mental health first aid classes again. How was a severely damaged brain able to do that? The thought that perhaps another powerful experience was occurring during my healing was rumbling around in me, taking charge of my life physically, mentally, emotionally, and spiritually—the healing hand of Jesus.

How else could it be explained?

Initially I was not 100 percent aware of His presence even though several people told me how much they prayed for my recovery, and believe me, I know their prayer played a huge role. I taught spiritual health coaching techniques in my natural healing work over the years, but in my own personal life there was always a little something missing. I've always believed that there are no accidents; events that happen to us are supposed to happen when they do. As a result of what has unfolded since my brain injury, I absolutely know it was supposed to be part of my earth school experience. Though I don't know all the reasons yet, my healing isn't an accident. I know I was helped by the little miracles that popped in to assist in the process.

When a miracle occurs, it comes at the right time if one is tuned in enough to recognize it. *A Course in Miracles* teaches that there is no order of difficulty in miracles. The only thing that matters is their source, which is often far beyond evaluation. Prayer is very much a medium of miracles. Most people think that a miracle must be a monstrous thing, but in fact the simplest, slightest of things, can create the most magnificent impact on one's life. It has happened to me several times...and the timing has been impeccable, along with the circumstances that caused it.

Backstory

From childhood to late middle age, there were countless times when the meanness and abuse from people I loved were intolerable. The shame and humiliation I felt most of my life drove me to search through the piles of compost to find love. Like other people, I built walls of protection, which only served to prevent me from reaching out and trusting.

I spent years studying and searching different philosophies to find joy, promise, and peace. I suffered many tragedies and spent too many years in agony and believed it was supposed to be my path to *mastery or enlightenment.* Yet I was saved countless times from destruction and a few times from actual death...including the day when my husband killed himself. (I will address this further in the book.)

Who was saving me? I was still here.

Why?

Had I achieved mastery yet?

Couldn't be. Mastery is supposed to feel joyful...peaceful...filled with unconditional love...and I wasn't experiencing any of those things. And yet...through it all, I was protected and survived, and I grew to know there was a Higher Power around me. I even gave this presence a name. It was *source energy.* Only rarely did I refer to this energy as God or Holy Spirit...never...JESUS.

During those years as I began awakening to my path of enlightenment, I knew an energy was always with me. When I was "tuned in," I could feel it. Quantum physics taught me that. But mostly, I gave credit to my protection from angels. My studies said that angels were God's helpers, and we all had them around us. I began the practice of saying thank-you to my perceived angel helper(s) throughout the day for the smallest positive event or miracle that occurred. Even though I didn't use them to answer prayers or worship them, I felt it was a step in the right direction.

As I delved deeper into my studies of consciousness or spirituality, I gathered with other seekers of enlightenment to study... like minds, etc. Still there were needs to be met, and I know now I was missing the signs I had been praying for. I kept trying to make things and people work in my experience. It didn't happen. Worked harder. I filled hundreds of pages in my journals. My computer is full of teachings from others I considered guides. Only a few sentences found their way in from a prophet named Jesus. Occasionally I typed or saved something He said. I knew His words were true, but I missed the most profound message: that Jesus was God in the flesh!

Then in the summer of 2019, a *crack* occurred that instantly got my attention, and it soon developed into a *chasm*. They say that timing is everything, but why does this magical timing take so long to happen?

Meanwhile, back to the crack.

As a result of teaching a mental health first aid class at Advent Health Hospital, an attendee named Kim Spear called me. She was a deacon at St. Edwards Episcopal Church locally and wondered if it might be possible to conduct a class for various members of the church. She and I made an appointment to meet to share information. It was during our phone conversation that Kim mentioned a group at the church called the Order of St. Luke Healing Ministry. (OSL). A little crack began to poke my heart.

I planned to share the outline for the eight-hour mental health class when we met. However, that never happened. Instead, I plied Kim with questions for forty-five minutes as she shared with me more about OSL and the healing miracles of Jesus. It was during Kim's sharing I experienced a profound realization. In the thirty years of spending my life studying different religions and eastern philosophies, I never studied Christianity. Why was that? How did I not know about miracles Jesus performed?

After this meeting with Kim, I knew my spiritual path was going to change. I wanted to join OSL and begin a program of study.

New Path

When the thought of becoming a member of OSL began to permeate my brain, so did several other concerns. Would I be good enough to fit in? I had often said a prayer for other people, but I didn't know about healing prayers that involved using Jesus's name. Then there was my ignorance of who Jesus really was, and why so many people worshiped Him. That prompted my concern about my level of faith in Jesus and the little faith I had in myself. Up to now I hadn't developed much of a relationship with Him. I had no clue about who He was, and what He came into the world to accomplish.

I didn't feel knowledgeable enough and was worried about the level of commitment involved. Afterall, I had yet to read the Bible cover to cover or study the Gospels. I'd spent the last many years steeped in the study of the eastern religions, quantum physics, and spirituality, and while I had attended and been confirmed in the Episcopal Church when I was younger, I hadn't stepped through the doors of one in over thirty years.

I blathered all this to Kim during our meeting, but Kim reassured me that I had nothing to lose to go ahead and sign up for the classwork involved, put my heart into it, and ask for guidance from the Big Guy—God—my words, not hers. She said, "If it doesn't work out, you will be led in another direction. It will be good because God only deals in good." Either way, Jesus would be pleased to add another lamb to His flock.

So that is what I did.

I signed up with OSL, paid my membership fee, and started my many months of study with Dr. Josh Acton, the North American director of OSL and his class, "The 26 Healing Miracles of Jesus

Christ" online. After I completed outstanding series, I enrolled in Dr. Kathleen Adams's (also in California) healing classes as well. She is a retired Episcopal priest. I also started attending St. Edwards Episcopal Church at 8:00 a.m. every Sunday. All this after stating boldly many times over several years that I was done with organized religion.

When I began the study of herbal medicine to become a practitioner of natural healing many years before, I was amazed by their healing capabilities. The study of the healing works Jesus did as God in the flesh on earth during His short three years surpassed my herbal study amazement. This caused my crack to slowly open into a chasm. I found myself hungry to master the teachings of some of the many great teachers and philosophers of biblical knowledge about God, Jesus, the Holy Spirit, and Christianity. Josh Acton and Dr. Kathleen opened doors I never knew were possible. Their knowledge of scripture, biblical history, and their personal relationship with Jesus as well as their online teaching presence fed my hunger. I found myself wanting to know more about the man who is our Lord and Savior.

It wasn't long into the coursework when I began to realize the *who* that I had known as *me* was changing. My brain was still healing from all the damage and trauma from injury and surgery, but even more so, because what I'd come to believe about spiritual truth from my past years of study was so completely opposite of or just plain wrong from what I was now being exposed to. My ignorance was glaring…and worse was the frustration I felt at believing I had wasted so much time in my life not knowing about or reaching out to the hand that was being offered to me the whole time.

I was opening to vulnerability.

PART II

Lessons That Helped Me Heal

Hope

During my childhood the monster didn't live under my bed. He lived in our house and sat at our table, raining abuse down on my mother, my brother, and me. He touched us physically, emotionally, and mentally. Not all the time. Every once in a while, he would disappear for a few months. He would go and spend time with other women. My mother, the *victim,* would then agonize over his being gone. Meanwhile, I felt a reprieve as anxiety and fear would temporarily loosen their hold on me. They never went away. But then the monster would call from some obscure place, and you can guess the rest. My mother would pack us up to chase after him. She *loved* him. She did not save us.

Hope did not exist.

My father and mother killed any *hope* of me having feelings of expectation or feelings of trust growing up. Certain kinds of trauma can do that to anyone, but especially a child. There was no safe place for me to hide nor words to help build a feeling of chance or optimism. I learned how to survive, but my *thrive* had a lot of holes in it.

When I was young, my experience of church was that of a drop off place. Other families would invite my brother and me to join them. They had *hopes* of saving us. They learned it was important to do that in their churches. I liked being there although I understood very little that was taking place. There was no consistency of belief until I became a teenager and was able to join a youth fellowship program in an Episcopal Church.

I was baptized as an infant, which meant I received an outpouring of the Holy Spirit, and many years later as a teenager I was confirmed in the church. At that point I really had no clue what any of that meant. It had little impact since I was still living in fear and abuse at home with my father, the monster, and his victim wife, my mother. Their dynamic wasn't changing, but as I grew, I was beginning to see a different future for myself. I was ready to get away from them, but it wasn't *hope* that was driving me. It was anger.

I became hardened against the word *hope* because it never worked. It only produced disappointing results. Worse, if the monster found out I was *hoping* for something, he would do his best to squish it like a bug. My mother was a perfect example of the failure of *hope*.

As I grew into a young adult, every now and then, the *hope* thing would wiggle its way into my life as little successes began to happen for me. I wasn't praying for them by asking Jesus or God because those two energies weren't in my consciousness yet. I still had a very strong "anti-self-worthiness" thing going on. It was easier not to hope for anything for myself. No expectations meant less rejection. I did feel it was okay to hope for my children. It worked better for them because I had a checkbook to fuel their wishes...sort of like Santa Claus.

Things are different now. My studies with OSL have brought me to a new place with the concept of *hope*. I didn't realize that hope could do many things. For example, I am now aware hope plays a critical role in my well-being and happiness. It motivates me to stop playing games with my previous *victim mentality* and get busy doing my forgiveness work or redirect it away from blaming someone else. For me, hope reflects that change is possible. It empowers me.

In addition, I am learning hope is more likely to come to fruition if God is the guiding force behind my ask. The voice of the Holy Spirit can step in and offer suggestions on what I need to do to make my request a reality. It can also take an opposite approach, which is to slow me down and add some patience and a healthier state of mind about my level of determination to make this hope thing happen. If it is right, I won't have to do anything because God will bring it to me without my interference.

Christianity teaches us there is a much bigger hope we need to focus on. It is the *blessed hope and promise of Jesus*. Many people refer to it as the Second Coming of Christ. N. T. Wright explains this very well in his book *Surprised by Hope*. Jesus's coming won't be about us dying and meeting Him in heaven, but rather that heaven will come to earth. The Lord's Prayer says, "God's Kingdom will come, and His will be done on earth as it is in heaven. Death will be defeated forever. Jesus, our living God, will live among us pouring out His grace on us. God's redeemed people will be living in this new world."

N. T. Wright referred to this event as *life after life after death*. Salvation is not in going to heaven but rather being raised to life in God's heaven on earth. The good news is, we can begin to bring the kingdom of God here *now* by fully living in the present, letting go of our lies and corruption. It means living consciously between the resurrection of Jesus and the hope of the new world to come by reflecting God's love for us and one another.

Forgiveness

Somehow during my late twenties, I developed the ideology of the "wolf pack" theory—only the strong survive and the weak get eaten. Terms such as *alpha, dominance,* and *control* entered my mental universe along with new patterns of thought and behavior. Thankfully, this approach to animal training has been radically disproved over time; and while abuse is still rampant, softer approaches are evolving.

Within me though, there was no *positive animal trainer,* and I was liking this new kind of power. Over time I became a force to be reckoned with…*a pack leader…*and the bullies and abusers began backing away. I received promotions in my work and eventually became a regional VP over a huge chain of health clubs. However, while I was exceling professionally, I struggled with personal relationships. Now I recognize it might have been because there was no room for compassion in my hard-held beliefs and absolutely no room for the act of forgiveness.

And here it is, that word *forgiveness*—the hardest task that all human beings who want to master becoming a true follower of Jesus will have to tackle and ultimately fail at.

I understood that actively practicing forgiveness and loving my enemies were going to be part of the package. Those were going to be difficult enough to accomplish, but I had no clue that the act of *unforgiveness* is the biggest block to healing an open, gaping emotional wound if I wanted to fully commit to Jesus. In my life I played the game of negotiation that we all try, "I can forgive that past situation or person, but not this one. Certainly, that will help me heal." It didn't, and I didn't understand why. I would ask God, "Why do I continue to allow this perpetrator to steal my joy, my life, my very existence?" I hadn't yet realized I had covered myself with a cloud so thick that no prayer could get through. In refusing to forgive, I literally handed over my mind, body, and spirit to someone or something else. My perceived perpetrator was joined to me, and that fed my anger and victim mentality. He or she did not deserve to be forgiven.

Life isn't fair, but the good and bad news is, none of us are more special than the other. I was finally glad to learn that what Jesus suffered on the cross gave me equal footing with everyone else. I am a child of Jesus Christ, anointed and loved. Self-esteem is needed if it doesn't develop an overbearing ego. While our ego is needed to navigate our human existence, it can also create problems. Our ego can be negative and controlling and work against us. It can present a daily challenge for forgiveness because it can tell us we are better than we are. It is protective of us. It doesn't want us to hurt while forgiveness wants us to accept pain, unleash the baggage, and move on. The ego often chokes on the words "I forgive you." Sometimes, you just have to *bless the hell out* of someone before you permanently remove them from your life.

I had to make a choice. I had to check my judgment and unwillingness to forgive. God holds nothing against me, so I don't need to hold anything against myself or anyone else. He is determined to save me from myself. At the same time, He can't do that until I do the forgiveness work. Blame is no longer an option. Forgiveness is a decision. This is going to be more difficult than singing to myself, "Jesus loves me; this I know for the Bible tells me so." I suspect this forgiveness thing is going to present a lifelong challenge.

Richard Bach (author *Jonathan Livingston Seagull*) wrote in his book *Illusions,* "If we want to end this lifetime higher than we began, we must expect an uphill road."

Faith

When I began my studies in OSL, the word *faith* was something I needed to seriously contemplate. I was faced with having to deal with a lack of understanding of what faith really means in being a Christian and following the teachings of Jesus Christ in His healing ministry. In the stories of the twenty-six healing miracles, Jesus healed total strangers. People he'd never met before. His desire and compassion were nondiscriminatory. However, He did notice the level of faith exhibited by the seeker. Some had much more than others, causing Jesus to add, "Your faith has made you well. Go in peace." Jesus didn't just deal with healing a physical ailment, but rather the whole person in spirit as well, which ultimately was his goal for everyone, including me.

It isn't unusual for people to use the terms *faith* and *belief* interchangeably, but there is a difference when speaking about God. Faith is the confidence that what God said will come to pass. Faith is not having giant wishes and then hoping God will make them come true. Faith is bigger than belief and requires *action*. It must be based on God's power. If you lack faith, you won't be able to do what God asks. In other words, without faith it is impossible to please God.

This brought me a huge level of concern. What level was my faith? Had I totally let go of my wolf pack belief yet? I couldn't develop faith in God and still hold onto my previous rigid mindset about empathy and compassion.

Up to now my life had not been about adjusting my life to do the will of God. To become faithful in Christianity means changing my belief. Belief that comes from the mind and may or may not include good works. Faith in God comes more from our hearts.

There is a cost involved. Faith is taking the next step first. I would have to leave my comfort zone, wretched as it was, to step into the unknown. What choice did I have? It was becoming clear to me I didn't want to stay where I was.

There is a necessary diligence to keep faith alive. The author C. S. Lewis says in his book, *Mere Christianity*, "One must train the habit of faith. That is why daily prayers and religious readings and church going are necessary parts of the Christian life. We have to be continually reminded of what we believe. Neither this belief nor any other will automatically remain alive in the mind." He went on to say that faith is the most difficult thing he tackled during the writing of his book.

The four gospels are full of stories throughout the New Testament of the risks Jesus and His followers took to spread the word of God. *God wants people whole.* How much change needed to take place in me was magnified by this statement: *God can feel what I am feeling.* If this is true, I have no place to hide. I don't even have to *take an action.* My thought is enough to do me in. OSL was teaching me that without faith in God, I would have a hard time in believing in anything of value. Our egos would like us to believe that we are powerful enough to do things on our own strength. With faith and our commitment to obey Him, God will tell us what to do. That is another great gift for our Christianity toolbox. It is sure a lot easier than trying to constantly figure it out on our own.

Prayer

There is a massive amount of information on the internet defining the word *prayer*. What it is…how to do it…who to do it for…what the qualifications are for the person doing the praying, and whether or not prayer is necessary for a happy life. The list goes on.

I never felt I was very good at saying prayers. It was always easier to pray for someone else other than myself, my children especially. My granddaughter, Gabby, was born at twenty-four weeks and weighed only one pound. For weeks, her life was in peril. My daughter called me at least four times when Gabby's life was hanging by a thread. She was in Florida. I was in Colorado. On those four occasions, I would go into my bedroom and get down on my knees and plead with God. I would stay there until my daughter called me back to tell me our baby girl was still hanging onto her frail little life. How did I know how to do that? There was a strong prompt from somewhere. Spirit prevailed and Gabby survived and has grown into a beautiful young woman. There have only been a few times in my life when I have asked God to help me through my agony or when my heart felt broken in half. I guess I didn't think I was worthy.

It turns out that I am because Jesus died for me.

The sad thing is, when I did pray, I never prayed to Jesus. After I said, "Amen," I didn't add, "In Jesus's name." I wasn't connected. Now I hold the belief that prayer is the *strongest tool* that anyone can have in their toolbox.

I've been mesmerized by the *prayer warriors* I've encountered during my OSL studies and the awesome words they seem to bring up from their big toes. It doesn't seem to matter the time or the location. They can step into this nonvisible world and touch the right nerve for the person(s) or situation(s) in need. I view this as a magical skill or art.

When I pray for someone to heal, Jesus knows…no matter my skill set. As I continue to build a relationship with God, I have come to realize the depth of His love for me. I am learning that prayer is not necessary for me to earn my way to heaven because Jesus has already done that for us when He died for us on the cross. So my quiet prayer is just as valuable as if spoken out loud if my heart is in the right place. Even if I don't consider myself to be a strong person of prayer, God will mold me if I have compassion and desire to help someone to heal.

OSL and my church has taught me that an important aspect of healing prayer is compassion. *Jesus is the human face of the compassion of God.* It is our spiritual obligation to pray for help of the suffering of others. But what do I do for me? How do I turn my own understanding, acceptance, and love inward? The self-judgment switch is always more on than off. One of my prayer practices is to ask God during my morning prayer, "to bring me to who You created me to be." It is one of the ways I attempt to get my Candace ego out of the way and let go of *her* control. God knows more about what my highest good for me is than I can ever know from my own perspective. I also ask Holy Spirit to speak to me, clarifying God's direction for me and to speak through me when I am speaking with others. It is not easy to control judgment or criticism. I like the added support from a more powerful influencer.

Spontaneous healing can be labeled as a miracle. It is healing without medical intervention. This happens more often than medical journals or big pharma care to disclose. There is proof to show that spontaneous healing of cancer can be due to the sudden onset of such a dynamic surge in the immune system activity that the cancerous growth is destroyed within days, sometimes within hours. Who is to say that *Jesus's healing hand* was not employed? Do not ever become discouraged. Keep the prayer coming.

One last point in this prayer chapter. My confusion over the various Christian teachings that *if I have a strong enough belief about what I ask for, I will receive it* because God wants to answer my prayers. Two questions I have learned to ask myself before I make the ask:

1. Am I asking for this (thing) because I want it?
2. Am I asking because God wants it for me?

This helps put my prayer into a better perspective when the "thing" doesn't show up or it is delayed for a long time.

The result is up to God's will, not mine.

Vulnerability

I grew up in a home that provided no tolerance for empathy or crying, or no safe place to express pain. I had no rights when it came to expressing grief over the death of my dog or feeling deep fear or wanting to be held, etc. It was made clear to me that crying was a weakness. I learned how to suppress my feelings. Grief, shame, fear, and low self-esteem festered. My survival instinct grew into protective walls making an impact on my ability to trust or develop social skills. It was difficult for me to build a meaningful relationship with just about anyone because I never understood why it was so difficult. I turned inward and began to build my "blame of self" package. I learned how to numb myself.

Through my studies on my path to becoming a practitioner of Christianity and follower of Jesus, I learned I must be willing to become vulnerable.

My avoidance bells were clanging! There had to be a way around this lesson. After all, there were risks involved in opening myself up, which included more possibility of being hurt. Asking for help requires vulnerability and the courage to face rejection. I had to understand there are no quick fixes without doing some tough work. Praying for help while facing thoughts of failure, I delved into the study of the pros and cons of vulnerability from a Christian perspective. I realized quickly I'd added a critical mass of negative attitudes and behaviors, which required an immense amount of undoing.

I had already learned that my flaws didn't stop God from loving me, so I felt safe to expose myself to Him. It was okay to be *wobbly*, just as a child taking their first steps. God would stabilize me. I was missing out on all the goodies that being vulnerable would help grow me. Here are a few: *more empathy and understanding, a huge increase in self-worth, decrease in all the negatives of fear, anger, feelings of lone-liness, worry, shame and guilt, etc. With the added attributes of vulner-ability, I would attract better people into my life and develop more trust and deeper connections. I would be willing to show more of my true self and feel free from the false self-syndrome I often hid in.*

I know now that vulnerability is a pathway to my finding strength in God to live out His purpose and build a bridge between me and my church. It helps me share my authentic self while no longer being concerned with someone judging me. When you accept that you are imperfect, courage is required when allowing your true self to be seen, but this is the only way so you can make a real connection with others.

Opening myself up allows me to be bold to ask questions of others if I see them struggling such as, "Are you okay?" or "Can I help you?" and the really uncomfortable one, "Can I pray for you?" Above all, I want to feel comfortable and confident in my walk and talk with God in the world. It has helped me to know that if I ask for Him, Christ's healing hands and the power of the Holy Spirit will be there to assist my prayer. This is important when you have no control over the outcome when you decide to put yourself out *there.*

It lets me know *I am enough just the way I am!*

Fear

Fear is Satan's number *one* tactic! It is designed to attack the *mind.*

The devil is always prowling around with his cadre of demons, ready to attack our thought with temptation or worse. Even many Christians believe Satan has the power to possess us, but NOT on God's word. The key is having a *true believer's spirit.* The salvation of Jesus protects us if we have faith.

Feeling fear is real. We've all experienced it in varying degrees, and sometimes it is necessary. Danger exists in our human reality, but overwrought, just plain wrong perceptions can turn minds into trembling mush when our thought is suffering from an overactive imagination. Fear can feel terrifying and exhilarating depending on the situation. It can mobilize or paralyze us into action or reaction. It can heal us or kill us over time.

We know that psychological stress can have a severe impact on the body's immune response. That is why when a cancer patient comes to see me for a natural health consultation, my first question is, "Where is your thought with this disease?" Thoughts of fear can negatively impact the body's immune response. Often, they respond they are afraid they are going to die, when in fact, most people heal from cancer than die from it. I then spend as much time with them talking about the *power of their thought and healing prayer* as I teach them about the amazing healing power of cancer-killing foods and natural remedies. If you aren't in control of your thought, something or somebody else is. That is a fact.

I have a tremendous amount of experience dealing with the impact of fear over thought since most of my life, fear was a persistent tyrant. Before I came to know Jesus, Satan had his nails into me. I was not Satan's willing follower, but he was my willing driver when it came to inundating my life with fear personally and professionally. He knew how to ding my low self-confidence, self-esteem, anger, and victim mentality buttons.

The amazing thing was, I was still able to excel professionally in spite of my oftentimes sheer terror of walking out the door of my house into the world. Over a twenty-year period, I progressed from being a fitness trainer. I was still able to excel professionally in a health club to becoming a regional vice president over seventy-two health club locations in Virginia, Baltimore, and South Jersey. My driving force had nothing to do with wanting to be successful. I was totally motivated by the *fear of failure*. I did my best to hide this from everyone.

A woman named Susan Jeffers authored a book entitled *Feel the Fear and Do It Anyway*. Her book was a powerful inspiration for me to continue facing my fear demons. Her quote, "The only way to get rid of the fear of doing something is to go out and do it." She added that what's important is to just act, and the confidence will follow. I still didn't know to use the voice of God/Jesus/Holy Spirit. I was following Susan's advice and stepping further out in the world and facing my fear obstacles, but my *confidence* gains were developing more slowly. Although Susan's book provided guidance in dealing with fear, her book, like the plethora of other self-help books that were beginning to flood the market in those years, did not go deep enough.

Fear is the dragon at the gate. Satan wants to excavate the soul. It is a fungus that grows in the dark places of consciousness, but it can only affect me when I allow it to close off the *word and light of God*. In other words, fear is only as strong as my avoidance to deal with it. Once I came to accept that fear does not come from God, I could stop inviting it in or creating it in my perception.

Failure can be a good thing...or a *God thing*. Even God has been known to use failure for us as a teaching tool. Failure can help reveal our sin. It can change our goals for the future by teaching us value in reaching for something beyond ourselves. If God is involved, we can reach deeper.

I wasted a good deal of my life feeling afraid because I didn't know how to talk to God or seek his guidance to bring me peace. Fear blocked my awareness of the role He could have played in my life. I only now imagine how the results could have been more spectacular without fear affecting my mind.

Isaiah 41:10 says, "Fear thou not; for I am with thee: be not dismayed: for I am thy God: I will strengthen thee: yea, I will help thee; yea, I will uphold thee with the 'right hand' of My Righteousness."

Truth

Truth is a verified, indisputable fact. For example, *God is only good.* He made us out of love for the purpose of sharing love so we can experience his goodness and reflect his image. God is always 100 percent!

Imagine the issues it would cause if we asked for God's mercy and in that moment, he is only 92 percent—or if he decides, as we often do in the middle of an important task, to take a break. *I'm feeling overwhelmed by these humans today. I'll get back to them later.*

Many of us might want to debate that it's *not* what God does, but who he is that matters. That should be true of us as well. I shouldn't be judged by what I do but rather by what is in my heart. It doesn't work this way in the world. My new question was, "How open is my heart to receive God's blessing?" Which then leads me to ask myself, "Why am I not doing more?"

Unfortunately, we can never be as holy as God.

Einstein said, "Whoever undertakes to set him/herself up as a judge of truth and knowledge is shipwrecked by the laughter of God." What is truth for us humans?

Christianity is teaching me that everything is better when I do it with Jesus. The blessing is that I don't have to have it all figured out. Holy Spirit will give me guidance if I listen. The challenge is overcoming the lies of the world and the ones Satan likes to plant in my mind to cause misdirection. He wants me to blame God when something goes wrong, but the truth is that God does not orchestrate tragedies. I can even find grace in my suffering when I let go of my *victim mentality* where blame likes to live. Sometimes the very thing I fight against is the hand of God trying to lead me into a new direction. There are times He will push me into an uncomfortable situation that forces me to use my faith. There is no *what* for God to know, He can show up in everything. I don't always like this, but the truth is, God loves me too much to leave me alone. That is how I felt as a mom with my kids, and they didn't always like it either. Instead of resisting God's truth, we can open to being shaped and molded by it.

This begs the question, "Why do bad things happen to good people?"

Because there are no good people! It took courage on my part to dare to write this line. We are not immune from *sin.*

All of us has said at one time or another, "So-and-so is a really good person." I've said it about my own self on occasion, and there are days when I am sure I get a kudo or two for meeting that expectation. However, other days I fail miserably for the slightest thing. For example, a new neighbor moved in next door to me. She was so very sweet, but then she began saturating her yard with ornaments like angels, gnomes, and an overabundance of plaster animals. This created in my mind a bunch of unattractive clutter. She hadn't bothered to trim any of her overgrown shrubbery. My heart was not thinking warm thoughts about her. I was judging her. Thought carries a lot of weight, and when I believe something, good or bad, I make it true for myself.

Is it possible to live in this world without telling a lie? Or just a little bitty fib? Jesus never had to lie for self-protection. He knew how to avoid the traps from His enemies. We don't always know how to do that. Even one of the commandments does *not* say, "Thou shall not lie." It says, "Thou shall not bear false witness." We translate this to mean that a lie that creates a consequence to hurt someone is a sin, but if a lie prevents irreversible damage, *the good consequence out ways the bad,* then the lie is more acceptable to us.

But is it to God?

There are degrees to our lies, *from fibs or white lies* we employ so we don't hurt someone's feelings (empathy, compassion), all the way to *black lies, which are a different story: designed for control or harm, manipulation, deceit, or survival.* I would say we use our perceived *good lies* when we want to be honest with someone, but not everyone wants honesty and not everyone has the courage to be honest. Even I sometimes add a caveat if someone asks me if they can be honest with me. I have been known to say, "Of course I want you to be honest with me, but can you please do it with kindness?" when I suspect a hammer is about to come down. I think all of us would prefer the word *nuance* to be involved when we are being criticized.

What is truth? No one set definition for us humans. I like the sound of this statement, "There is a lot of handwashing going on in the world today, when it is more important to keep our soul clean." What bad lie do I hold about myself today that I can change? What do I want my truth to be?

God's Purpose

When I turned forty, I left my job in the health club industry after nearly twenty years. At the same time, my husband and I decided to make a huge life change to relocate to the mountains of Colorado. We opened a consulting business and combined our skills in writing, communication, and management. While I loved the writing projects, I did not enjoy the consulting work. It was not fulfilling. I was used to instant gratification when working with my health club clients. I always enjoyed sharing in their excitement when they achieved various fitness goals. I felt frustrated when working with unmotivated individuals in these companies. But above all, I felt no sense of *purpose.*

The idea of a new purpose constantly gnawed at me. It occurred to me to ask God to help me find my new *who.* Actually, it was more like begging. Sometimes I would cry. One day, a catalog appeared in the mail from a college offering classes in alternative medicine. I did not order this catalogue. I read through the requirements and coursework and was very intrigued but tossed the catalog aside anyway. I was a great example of someone pleading for answers and then not recognizing the gift when it was presented.

Still suffering and thinking about options, I bought a book entitled, *Zen and the Art of Motorcycle Maintenance* by Robert M. Pirsig. It was the story of a man's quest for truth—the way to think and feel about life. The cycle you work on is yourself to achieve inner peace of mind. By the time I read and completed all the exercises in the book, the light bulb in my heart came on...*my purpose.* It was not an accident that I remembered the catalogue from the college of natural health many months before. I contacted them for information and immediately signed up for classes. I was hungry to begin my new path in helping people heal with nutrition and natural healing remedies. It was a great follow up on for all my years dealing with health and fitness. I should say, *my purpose found me.* God answered my prayer on His schedule. It just took my human mind longer to realize it what *God's purpose was for me.*

What is *God's purpose* all about? Christianity teaches that God speaks to me through the Holy Spirit when He has a purpose in mind for my life. As much as I might pray for an answer, God chooses His own timing. That is my frustration to deal with. Maybe He was offering ideas, opportunities, or solutions sooner, and I wasn't tuned in to hearing His voice.

Every one of us is a part of God's creation, but it makes sense that if we are in relationship with Him, we can hear His voice more clearly. I wasn't in relationship with God, His Son Jesus, or the Holy Spirit while I was pitifully *begging to know my purpose.* I was busy working the world's purposes. God is not interested in being my cocreator. He wants to lead and me to follow.

When my son Max was fifteen, he announced he wanted to be a Navy pilot. Amazingly, he succeeded in that endeavor and paid them back with a ten-year commitment required as a result of his outstanding training. When he left the Navy, JetBlue opened a door for him. He has been a captain with JetBlue for the last seventeen years. I recently asked Max if he remembers about his motivation to succeed and if he had ever doubted his decision after all these years. He replied, "Once I became a part of the Naval ROTC program in college, I was surrounded by motivated individuals with the same goal I had. It encouraged me to maintain a highly relentless attitude to succeed." He further shared, that of course, he certainly had some occasional thoughts of *fear of failure* and the desire *not to let anyone down,* which helped to push him through the tougher challenges. He said he never sensed a *higher power* as a driving force...then. Now that he is older and a father of two children, his awareness has grown, and he now believes there was always another *energy* at work around him. When I asked him if he ever prays and thanks God, he answered, "All the time." We did have to debate about his word *goal* and my word *purpose* because I choose to believe a goal is something you aim for outside yourself, and your purpose is what drives you from inside, i.e., *the hand of God.* I believe, eventually, Max will come to believe that his careers with the Navy and JetBlue were no *accident.*

I completed all the requirements to become a naturopathic doctor and opened my natural healing practice. I was excited to work with my *new purpose.* I say it that way because purpose can change many times throughout our lives as we adapt to changes whether forced or chosen. It was important for me *now* to be a part of something bigger than myself. I think most of us recognize how wonderful it is to be involved in an undertaking where the mind is so completely absorbed, we forget our surroundings and ourselves. This is often called *being in the flow or a state of mindfulness.* How much does that come from inside us versus an innate force called *intuition or the voice of the Holy Spirit or being endowed by God's purpose for us?*

Jesus teaches us in John 5:19, "I tell you the truth, the Son can do nothing by Himself; he can do only what he sees his Father doing, because whatever the Father does the Son also does. ... For as the Father has life in himself, so he has granted the Son to have life in himself."

Jesus also said in John 15:7, "If you abide in Me, and My words abide in you, you will ask what you desire, and it shall be done for you."

I wish I had known Jesus and been abiding in me all that time that I was busy crying and pleading. I had wrong expectations of God because I hadn't adjusted my own, or to put it mildly, *God was waiting for me to get my act together.*

God's Grace

God's grace was new to me. It sounded good but left me with a lot of questions. I found out that most Christians know what it means to have this special "grace," yet I had no clue if I had it. The key was who to ask those who would have the best answer. So...back to my mentors Kim Spear and further on to Fr. Mark Lafler, my priest, and my good spiritual friend, Marsha Huertas. Here are some things I found out:

What is God's grace? It is divine influence filled with love and mercy given freely. It is unmerited favor available to all who are in Christ. Without God's grace we cannot live gloriously in life. Grace means forgiveness from the Trinity...God, Jesus, and Holy Spirit... so we are victorious over our sin.

Why is it important? It is important because we are all sinners even when we try our hardest not to be. To compound the problem, sinning is inevitable because it includes everything we think, say, and do. This is a constant burden we all bear because practicing Christianity is *not* for the squeamish. There is always another lesson.

Who deserves it? They all said, "None of us, but we are given it anyway because Jesus paid the price for our sins.

Grace is a promise from God. It is a gift we can't earn. We don't have to worry about being good enough for God even though we always fall short. It is eternal love that our sins can never destroy. In addition, my research taught me that grace is an active power that protects us. It is that *still small voice* speaking to us from the Holy Spirit that guides us and inspires us to follow God's will instead of the wrong messages we can receive from our own free will. Satan always likes to play with us.

I didn't feel right about this gift. I argued, "Why should people who commit the most grievous of sins still get grace?" I shared a list of examples from my own life while leaving out some of my own dastardly past deeds, of course. I was still experiencing some guilt and shame and feelings of unworthiness in being awarded this powerful gift of grace. My perceptions were skewed. It was like entering a room I was already in.

Eventually, my studies, practices, and teachers helped me make headway and believe that Jesus came to live in me and fill me with God's grace because *I received Him* in my life. It is a protection for our soul when we live in the Spirit of God. He created each one of us in His image. We are not mass-produced or ordinary. He calls each one of us a *masterpiece.*

Surrendering to God

A man named Abraham Maslow published a paper in 1943, *A Theory of Human Motivation,* which remains a popular framework in sociology and psychology instruction today. Maslow completely believed that *self-actualization* was possible in a person—a supreme human capable of becoming everything. Last on his hierarchy list was his belief in spiritual needs—giving credit to something larger than self but only after our basic needs had been met. He didn't think that religious experience was valid. There is no God in Maslow's hierarchy. He was a lifelong unyielding atheist.

Biblically, we know that all our human needs can be met with God, but how easy does it sound to *let go and let God?*

While my new brain was forming, I was not conscious of choosing much of anything on my own. I was being and doing what was placed in front of me by others, some who were caring and others not so much. You might say I was completely surrendered to God. Why? Because I know now that God was in charge. He was guiding my inner thermostat and timing without my awareness. It was not a smooth ride by any means. My behavior was often bizarre…initially I couldn't tell good from bad, a lie from truth. I was suffering from PTSD terrors, and my broken brain made it hard for me to feel God's presence.

As weeks turned into months during my studies, adjustments were taking place in my thoughts, my perceptions, and viewpoints from the past. It was hindering my progress. As my brain mind and heart mind started to gel, I realized it was doing me no good to dwell on the past, and what I couldn't change. God gave me a miracle of healing. It was time I started to live in gratitude…to consciously move into the present moment and surrender to Him.

Holy Spirit delivered a personal message from God to me. He said, "It's okay, Candace. You aren't invisible, I see you."

Part of the joy of surrendering to God is the constant little signs He sends to let us know how valuable and loved we are. He doesn't break our hearts, abuse us, or leave us in fear. Instead, he surrounds us in *holy instant moments* of joy and peace. But we must do our part. God is seeking absolute surrender. In the beginning, this can feel like a huge sacrifice because we have a lot of *undoing* to do. Belief and trust are critical components in the process.

Trust can be particularly difficult because it involves believing in something you can't see. It involves a probability that someone will behave in a certain way and creates confidence or willingness to share a relationship with another person.

While I was walking with my neighbor, Charlene, this morning, I asked her to explain her belief and experience with trust. Her answer was so completely different from my experience. She started by saying, "It was natural. I never thought about it. I felt safe as a child with people. I just seemed to trust everybody." Wow! I thought to myself, but then I remembered that her father was a pastor of a church. She grew up already surrendered to God. She was indoctrinated at a very early age to take her worry and fear to God. How do we build trust in God when you grow up the way I did, with the belief that others can't be trusted?

Scripture says we start by paying attention because if we listen, *Holy Spirit* will give us direction in obeying God. If we choose to do that, it can mean a lot of change, we might not be prepared for. A question I had to ask myself was, "How much am I willing to yield to God to follow Him?" This was not going to be an overnight process for me. What do I do with my free will and my ego, which so badly wanted to stay in charge? The truth is that God is the only one living fully in us in the present moment where He wants us and where He seeks us. Our free will allows us to choose the demon or God's powerful healing voice.

God's grace also provides us with an occasional *AHA moment (a tiny miracle)* when we might feel tinged with a feeling of *enlightenment*...a moment of great knowing or understanding, which we know we didn't cause, but the ego so loves to take credit for. We should not become so stimulated by one of these mysterious events to let it elevate our thinking that God and I are now the same person. How else would this answer have come to me? Zen Buddhism teaches that even the enlightened Zen master still needs his rice every day.

Isaiah 55:9 gives us a goal to aim for: "As the heavens are higher than the earth, so are my ways higher than your ways, and my thoughts than your thoughts."

I could only start with baby steps, and most days, that is still the best I can do, but I am on the path to surrendering.

I recently asked a few friends at church if they thought they were fully surrendered to God. Some of their answers were quite comical.

They are all trying too.

Love

How special am I?

Pretty special because God loves me unconditionally.

This is a big gift. Are there strings attached to this? That word *unconditionally* sounds challenging.

I can't remember ever having been given unconditional love from another human being not because a few of them didn't want to give it. It just wasn't hardwired into them nor was it in me to return it. I think most of us believe only our dogs love us that way in spite of our stupidity or abuse. Cats are smarter. They have keener awareness about us humans…just as God does, but God wields a bigger hammer. He is the King of forgiveness and holds a large bag of many chances.

I've heard zillions of people say they love their children unconditionally. They would gladly and without hesitation jump in front of a train for them. I went through a phase of that when my children were babies and toddlers. Then the disease of *teenager* happened, and I started suffering the slings and arrows of their judgment and anger of me as their mom when I failed their expectations. I still loved them, yet they were biting me. Their behavior was no longer cute. They could make me cry. Unconditional love was taking on a different hue.

What is our level of motivation regarding the need for *relationship* with other humans? When asked, most people will say their greatest fear is *being alone*. Some can't even fathom living without a mate or a spouse. Who or what is the driving force for some people to continually seek peace and joy in a relationship with another after a loved one leaves through divorce or death, etc., while others find contentment in living alone? The difference between feeling lonely and being alone is *emotional attachment*. Where is God at this point in their lives? What is their definition of unconditional love now?

Agape (the Greek term for the fatherly love of God for humans, and the human reciprocal love for God) is the transcendent highest form of unconditional love. This statement is so overpowering as humans we can't even grasp its meaning. God gives this kind of love to us and would like us to reflect this back to Him. In fact, He created a commandment that says, "Love the Lord with all your heart and all of your soul and all of your strength." Jesus teaches this the first and greatest commandment.

All of God's commandments are choices. That is why we get into trouble. God does not force us to love Him, or in fact to obey any of the ten commandments. He empowers us. He provides stimulus through the Holy Spirit. God wants us all to be like His son Jesus.

Meanwhile Satan is always whispering in our ear, "Don't do it! Becoming a Christian is too much work." By the way, when you are important to God, you are precious to Satan. Think about that for a moment.

God does not need our love. He *wants* it...and the joy I am experiencing now that I recognize God wants a relationship with me is awesome. That void I mentioned earlier in this little book is diminishing as my love for God, Jesus, and the Holy Spirit is growing. I can feel my heart being purified so I can better reflect more of God's attributes as my relationship with Him is growing.

When we are in love with the Trinity, we have everything we need. My full-time job is to never allow my heart to question God's love for me.

PART III

More Challenges

Duality

Ego vs. True Self

The second we are born we begin to develop a personality referred to by psychologists as the *Ego (flesh self)*. As we grow and learn how to meet the demands of parents, caretakers, teachers, friends, and the world, we become creatures of our life experiences. Everyone has an ego, even the spiritual masters among us. It's not about losing the ego. It's about having the awareness to control it when it surfaces with harmful advice.

The *who* we build from opinions, speculations, teachings, etc. of others is a *false self* if God is not involved. While our egos are sometimes necessary to protect us from harm, the ego is often full of insecurities, fears, and doubts that influence our feelings of self-worth and self-confidence. This can cause us to adopt negative patterns of behavior and a wrong perception of self and life experience. However, the ego can also develop a *strong sense of self-worth*, which can cause us to take on false beliefs. For example, we might be more special than someone else. Then we find ourselves fully entrenched as human beings living in the duality or opposition with our spiritual or God self.

Because God created us, He put His Spirit in us before we were born. God is already *installed* in a baby's consciousness at birth. The Bible says children were planned by God and existed before their creation in His mind and heart. "Before I formed you in the womb I knew you, and before you were born, I consecrated you" (Jeremiah

1:5). They are fully human when still in the womb. Little children have a simple trust and dependency and their hearts are open—that is, until the ego begins to worm its way into their minds and drown out God's voice in order to take control.

Research is all over the lot about when a child develops the concept or ability to perceive *Spirit or free will* or begins to develop an *ego presence*. Children begin to use their free will to do what they can envision. However, they are limited in capability, capacity, and control. Children are influenced by the morals and ethics of their caregivers to learn the difference between right and wrong, but they still don't have the underlying emotions, feelings, beliefs, and impulses to help them understand what they are sensing. In fact, at a very young age, all children learn the terms *NO, ME, MINE,* and the expectation to be the *center of the universe,* already making the ego feel very happy. As they grow mentally, children develop a perspective to look at things, but not the ability to understand someone else might see the situation differently.

God's Spirit can't be changed because it is already *perfect.* Our mind must decide which *voice* it wants to serve. The ego wants us to believe we can create ourselves. It does its best to draw us away from choosing the Trinity to lead us. Ego uses many tools, and one of the strongest is the denial of truth that we are already perfect in the eyes of God. It wants us weak and afraid. It wants to distort our thoughts so it can control us...make us codependent. It seeks to serve itself and uses a lot of variation in behavior and judgment because our ego is unstable. Ego is mortal and Spirit is eternal. Our spirit seeks inner authenticity through God, Jesus, and the Holy Spirit. Ego seeks outward recognition, dominance rather than tolerance.

There is no variation in God because He has no ego. There is no place that God is *not.* Therefore, He is in each one of us, which means, we are connected to one another.

The ego only sees separation.

Ego is in direct competition with God. It is a wrong-minded attempt to get us to see ourselves as we wish to be rather than who we really are. Imagine how wonderful the release and deep peace we will know when we no longer live in the struggle of duality in our

mind and truly know our *spiritual self* and others without judge-
ment or separation. It is a daily effort to shut out the voice of the
ego. I ask the Holy Spirit to speak through me and drown out the
constant nagging of the ego to make me think *I am my body.* I try to
practice the thought "Namaste—my soul honors your soul" when I
encounter a stranger. Not always, because sometimes my ego enjoys
the famous line, which made it a movie star from the original *Top
Gun* movie when Mavericks's commanding officer said to him, "Your
ego is writing checks your body can't cash!"

God's joy is complete when ours is. He experienced it when
Jesus was fully home in the kingdom of heaven. He surrounds us
with love, protection, and charity. The Second Coming of Christ
means the ego's reign will be over. Our mind will be healed. The ego
can't share what it does not believe, and it does not believe in the
thoughts of God. We must pay attention.

Suicide Debris

(I mentioned in the first chapter that my husband killed
himself. I am going to share a bit of my experience
with his suicide and the leftovers that followed.)
Suicide is deliberately injuring yourself enough to die.

Some suicides are impulsive acts. Others are not. My husband's
suicide was not impulsive. "Yes," one of my friends said, "but did he
really wanna fuckin' die?" Sorry for the graphic comment, but that is
the way she talked.

Yes, he wanted to die. The last six weeks of his life was a play
of vacillation—going back and forth with an extreme desire to kill
himself, to dealing with his mental state of mind as he told me one
morning, "I really do want to kill myself, but I am afraid of dying."
That explains why he spent hours researching the perfect method for
himself. I found all this out by going through his computer after he
was gone. If you are remotely ignorant about the vast quantities of
information you can find out when researching the word *suicide*, you
might be shocked. Not only is there a litany of methods explained in
detail but also plenty of encouragement to spur people on. My husband chose *asphyxiation*. He hung himself from a telephone pole in
our backyard. It wasn't messy, and it didn't physically hurt.

Now, before your judgment bells go off about me, his wife, and
what I would have, could have, or should have done during his weeks
of deliberations, let me assure you, I wasn't sitting around twiddling
my thumbs. I've already written another book filled with the trauma
and gory details for myself and my dead husband.

Miley Cyrus recorded a song about a *wrecking ball*. I was riding one and couldn't get off.

Suicide is not the kind of death one feels comfortable discussing openly with others. As a bereaved spouse, even if we are innocent, we feel guilty. It is a disgraceful kind of death. The toxin that was eating me alive was shame. He was the one who killed himself, yet I was the one that felt ashamed. It took me the better part of two years after he was dead to be able to lift my head up around other people, and that was after working with a therapist. Guilt and shame are the two most useless emotions for us humans to endure along with the stupid questions you get asked by stupid people. "Oh, was he depressed?"

So...where was *God* in all of this?

Before my husband died, we both had been studying and following different spiritual paths. We would converge now and then for discussion. His God was different from my God. I had what I thought were comfortable beliefs about death, the afterlife, God, prayer, angels, *yada, yada, yada*. I felt I had God figured out. At 4:30 a.m., the day after my husband's death, I was standing out in my driveway staring at the telephone pole. I felt compelled to tell God that I was going to leave Him for a while. I had to go and figure myself out and that eventually, I was sure, I would return. At that most extreme time in my human experience, God was not my fallback position. I was sure He would be fine without me and go about His daily God business.

One thing I do remember thinking not long after the event was that I could choose to make my husband's shocking death my Vietnam and be a victim indefinitely or choose to make the rest of my life spectacular. I had absolutely no idea where to begin. I am writing this twenty years later.

One of the roles I've assumed these past many years is teaching mental health first aid. This is a federally funded program specifically designed to teach communities and professional organizations the topic of suicide. Classes usually include between fifteen to thirty students. Most often, the classes will include people who either have had direct experience with someone who died by suicide or know someone who has attempted (and on rare occasions someone will share that included him or herself specifically). Their opinions are varied about spiritual and religious aspects of the morality for someone to kill themselves. Because I am limited to the fidelity of the program, we can't spend any time unpacking that part of the discussion. But there is much consternation and frustration in the class with some of the church philosophy on the subject, which creates confusion and conflicted emotions.

Do people have a right to kill themselves? Does suicide automatically doom them to hell? Is there still a chance they will go to heaven?

As the moderator, I can't and don't share my opinion. Because of the leftover debris following my husband's suicide and my ensuing trek into the study of Christianity, I too felt the need to dig into what the truth is. I can't speak for what other churches teach. The internet will do that for you, as they are quite varied between what religion and spirituality teach. There are over seven billion people on the planet with seven billion different personal perceptions and beliefs along with different experiences of reality.

The Catholic Church is very clear that it holds suicide as a *very grave matter*. The church teaches that one's life is the property of God, and we have no right to destroy life. It is *sinful*.

The Bible says that only God gets to pass final judgment. However, there is still an opportunity to be saved. If we believe in Christ, we are guaranteed eternal life, and nothing can separate a Christian from God's love.

My husband was raised as a Christian Scientist. I never heard him speak of Jesus while we were married. But even I don't know what was in his mind or heart during the last seconds of his life as he was putting the rope around his neck. No one knows if he was speaking to God or Jesus before his body was dead.

What if he was repenting before he slid into unconsciousness?

PART IV

Finishing Up

Why Did My Brain Come Back Different?

Norman Cousins, professor of biobehavioral sciences and author said, "The human brain is a mirror to infinity. There is no limit to its range, scope, or creative growth once the full potential of mind is developed." That sounds awesome. Yet my brain was horribly injured.

As I look back at the healing process, it felt like my brain was always in the present moment because my past and future were missing. I was just *being*. That has changed now even though I have trained my new brain to stay focused heavily in the present moment...*where God is*.

I had no concept there was potential for me to heal. The blessing was, I had no idea how sick I was between my brain and total paralysis on my left side. My son, Max, was dedicated to helping me to stay focused on healing without truly knowing if I could or not. Most of the few people I had contact with during those months believed I would die. He made a promise to me, "Mom, I will never leave you, but you have to do everything you can to get well." I had no clue what he meant the many times he would add "when you get your brain back" during our phone conversations as the months passed.

My boundaries of self were in a state of flux because my internal compass was not familiar with the confusing perceptions and emotions I was experiencing with the outside world. I am sure this created chaos for friends I was previously close to. I lost a few who didn't have the inclination or patience to stick with me. They weren't the ones changing... My reality was. Many people suffering with

PTSD symptoms can relate. Just because I couldn't see it, it didn't mean it wasn't real.

As I said in the beginning, I was dealing with frequent brain seizures. I don't know how many because I don't have my medical records from the hospital. My skull was full of staples holding chunks of bone together. In addition, I was not very responsive to my caretakers poking and prodding me and issuing demands for my cooperation. I was labeled *non-compliant.* Some of them were nice to me. Others were Nazis! I still have tissue damage in my legs from the rough way I was handled. Fear was my primary emotion and very much a part of my experience. I had no advocate to watch out for me.

I began to recognize I had to be stronger than the damage that was being done to me by others in charge of my care via their insensitivity, lack of compassion, and patience. Unfortunately for me, a former very close friend is included in this group while I was in my first rehab, still suffering brain seizures. She thought I needed a jolt of reality to awaken to her perceived reality for me. She delivered this merry message when she came to visit me on Christmas Day. She told me matter-of-factly that I was basically doomed to live in a full care center: "This is the best it is going to be for you. You had better get used to it." She probably thinks I don't remember the imprint. If she wanted to destroy any feelings of hope on my part, it worked. It also increased my feelings of helplessness and fear exponentially. I had no brain power at the time, so I couldn't argue with her.

Still, I survived.

For most of the first three years of my new brain development, I was slowly exposed to memories and patterns of habits and relationships that were part of the *old Candace.* New possibilities were emerging, but my brain was still working to achieve a new *normal* and not giving me a lot of guidance for change in how to alter what she (old Candace) viewed as *reality.* God was not a strong component in her view of life and world.

After *God stepped in to help me,* my consciousness started to wake up. Along the way, the *voice of the Holy Spirit* wormed its way into my heart and brain. I came to realize a lot of people were praying for me. I believe *Jesus laid his healing hand on me* because my spirit became infected with encouragement to build a new model of the old Candace.

I am claiming this scripture for me written by Paul in 2 Corinthians 5:17, "Therefore, if anyone is in Christ, he is a new creation; old things have passed away; behold all things have become new." I am sure the ego isn't happy. It had me in its clutches and then lost hold.

Joe Dispenza, student of quantum physics and a wonderful spiritual teacher, wrote a book entitled *Your Immortal Brain*. "It has been calculated that there are more possible connections in one human brain than there are atoms in the universe." If this is true, mankind didn't create this amazing machine. Only God could have. Joe also said, "The brain contains as many neurons as there are stars in the Milky Way...about a hundred billion."

Hello, God

This amazing information caused me to do more research on why my brain healed to be different than it was before the subdural hematoma knocked me silly. The term *neuroplasticity* popped up in my brain studies. It means, "the ability to rewire and create new neural circuits at any age—to make substantial changes in the quality of life." Simply put, this allowed my brain to come back different, to cause a change in my perception of the world and people around me...indeed, to create a new reality and new beliefs. In other words, the brain can be rewired in certain instances, and we can incorporate new knowledge and experiences into our brain.

So do you still think that God did not have a role in my brain coming back different or...coming back at all?

Consciousness and Thought

Consciousness is the ultimate and intimate connection with God. People create their lives and world with or without God based on their beliefs. They can only imagine the possibilities and abilities the size of a pea or the super extraordinary universe based on their relationship with God. The Bible teaches us, "Behold the kingdom of God is within you" (Luke 17:21). If you believe!

The term consciousness frustrates many scientists because it can't be measured. Quantum physics teaches it is another form of reality—another form of energy. For me, God is the supreme source of all energy. Spirituality teaches *everything* comes from consciousness and God.

Where is God now in the nature of my mind? How much of a role does God have in my healing and creating my new sense of self?

Shakespeare said, "There is nothing good or bad but thinking makes it so!" It is the reception I give it mentally and the attitude I carry in my own thought that will completely determine its effect upon me.

Buddha taught that all we are is the result of what we have thought. The mind is everything. What we think we become. Mind isn't matter, but thought seems to be able to create matter.

I can be a victim or an empowered, enlightened individual simply by the kind of thought I choose to produce. The universe will serve up the answer. A victim will say or think, "It's not my fault. Poor me. I would never create that!" An enlightened person might say, "What am I doing, or not seeing, that caused this to happen?"

The way we think affects the brain. Kinesiology teaches that every thought creates a biochemical reaction, which acts as a chemical message to produce a feeling to match the way you are thinking. Happy thoughts equal happy chemicals such as *dopamine* or *serotonin* (*neurotransmitters*). The more we produce any kind of thought—good or bad—we create our *state of being*. Thoughts then become matter in our own bodies. And we become a self-perpetuating mechanism of our own misery and frustration or our joy and peace. God sets up our brains to adapt to respond to mental focusing. We can learn how to influence change in our behavior, thinking, and neural networks. There is plenty of proven science that thoughts are real, and we know thoughts directly affect our body. We can't just think ourselves into change. There comes a time for action.

The previous paragraph is a simple explanation. I used to teach a series on how you can learn to change your brain's wiring by changing your thought. I know this has been a factor in helping me focus on the *positive* messages coming to me from the Holy Spirit, often referred to as my *God voice*. I had to pray for help to make a new mind.

I believe that how I view God in my world is how my world is going to come back to me. I need to look for the meaning in what I am creating in my experience with my thought and action. Who or what is creating my reality if not God? Which guest am I inviting in?

Neuroscience teaches that it takes no more effort to form a positive thought than it does to form a negative one. Jesus said, "As the heavens are higher than the earth, so are my ways higher than your ways and my thoughts greater than your thoughts" (Isaiah 55:9).

The Power of Change

Is change ever an accident?

Sigmund Freud's most famous quote centers around the fact that *there is no such thing as an accident.* He went on to say, "It is not an accident if it is deliberate." However, his theories never included the *hand of God* as an intervener. Throughout his life, Freud was an uncompromising atheist. He regarded God as an illusion.

Jesus came to earth on a spiritual mission. His death on the cross was not an accident, but a moral necessity. He came here to save us, not to reign as an earthly king. Jesus said, "I came down from heaven not to do my will, but the will of Him that sent me" (John 6:38). He became obedient to death. He knew the cross was the end of His earthly journey, and the foretaste of a new beginning for salvation.

There is a difference between Jesus's experience and mine except for the fact that both our events caused *change.* His was through the *power of intention,* and mine, which at the time, seemed to be because of an accident.

I no longer believe my brain injury was an accident because of the incredible healing and spiritual transformation I have experienced. *Opening to Jesus was not an accident.*

I am focused on building a *new model* of Candace by mastering my thought so I can change self within. God places seeds in my consciousness and waits for me to grow them. It is up to me to create an environment or allow a condition to manifest the result. It is a daily challenge. The Bible says that Jesus taught *right thinking.* Every thought bears a signature. It continues until we realize potential. We didn't come from nothing. We are a continuation.

There is nothing between me and God. I was born with Him in my memory and His word in my heart. My job in earth school is to remember Jesus came here as *God in the flesh* to help open my mind and overcome *death*. God created me to be *eternal*. Jesus gave me the gift of *resurrection, a gift of reawakening*, from the illusion of this life so I would know the true meaning of *reality*. I don't have to wait for my body to die to live fully with God, Jesus, and the Holy Spirit. They are already with me.

Dr. Wayne Dyer teaches us in his book *The Power of Intention* to say out loud, "I'm not from here," just as Jesus said He was in the world, but not of it.

Joseph Campbell taught that eternity is now! Right now! Because we are infinite beings. Our infinite soul lives on.

What is my sense of destiny now? Have I tuned into my greater self yet?

Yes—for sure, a better self. I still have work to do. I must remind myself every day that my true nature is eternal. This inspires me to appreciate each moment of my life and give gratitude to the Trinity.

Deepak Chopra encourages in his book *The Future or God* to shout, "I am pure potential. I am pure possibility," as a part of my daily devotional.

Eckhart Tolle, in his book *The Power of Now*, says, "A fundamental thing to realize is that life is *now*! It is never not *now*! It is only this moment ever."

Proverbs 3:5–6: "Trust in the Lord with all thine heart; and lean not until thine own understanding. In all thy ways acknowledge Him, and He shall direct thy paths."

I can only experience pure consciousness in the present moment with God, Jesus, and Holy Spirit within me.

... A N D   T H E N

God

stepped in

My Journey Through Healing

SOME PRAISE FROM MY READERS

"In this heartfelt and inspiring book, Dr. Candace Booth takes her readers on a journey of Hope. A beautiful story of God's restoration and relentlessness to reconcile his creatures back to himself out of his great love for them. This memoir is a story of a life filled with emotional and physical suffering only to find that healing is found in Jesus Christ the Great Physician, Healer of body, mind and spirt."

Rev. Kimberley Spear, deacon, member of the Order of
St. Luke Healing Ministry, hospital chaplain

"This book is a must-read invitation to witness the miracle of healing. A serious brain injury, encountered by the author left her in a place of spiritual darkness with little faith. She decided to reach out to Jesus by prayer and by the will of God and through the power of the Holy spirit was healed. This spiritual healing caused a transformation and put her on a path to Christianity and a life made new. Reading this life changing powerful testimony, you will see God's will through the power of the Holy Spirit can do all things. Cure a brain injury, change a life, and make a non-believer become a believer. It can change your life too."

Rev. Robert E. and Karin J. Damon

"As I read this book, my heart is in 'awe' at the hand of God in Candace's life! Having known her since 2010, I have seen her life challenges. How wonderful it is to see how she has transformed her life! Her ability to express with such creative words & detail, keeps the reader relating yet wondering what's next. As she says in her book, 'my flaws didn't stop God.' The miracle of her health being restored is such an encouragement to me. My heart is that it will be for all who read this book. Thank you, Candace, for having the 'courage' to write about your life experiences & 'willingness' to press forward with your purpose in life."

Marsha Huertas, biblical teacher

"A few years ago, in my journey with Jesus, I decided that everything is either a blessing or a lesson. Without using the same words, I see that you are walking a similar path. Jesus Christ our Lord is ours as we are His. We don't have to earn His Love and Grace because they are freely given. Nor can we behave in a way that will separate us from it. You bring out this message very well in this book. Blessed by my sister in Christ Jesus."

Karyl Lou, MEd, OSL anointed healing minister
of By His Grace Healing Community

"I have known Candace for over twenty years. I thought I knew her well. After reading this heart rendering journey of her devastating brain injury and her miraculous resurrection, now I can say I know her well. This is her story of surviving and emerging as a new-born soul, who came to know God and connect with Jesus Christ never to be separated from His grace and mercy again."

Mary Zauche, cousin by marriage and friend

"The first time I saw my sister with a severe brain injury was two weeks after her surgery. She was suffering severe brain seizures and in and out of consciousness. I was scared to death for her. I did not think she would make it home again. My wife Mary and I are so amazed how her brain healed and the story she wrote of her healing journey. I am grateful for her many friends, and especially for her son Max, who supported her along the way as she gained a strong relationship with Jesus."

Mark and Mary Booth

About the Author

"There is no physical body, no matter what the state
of decline, no matter what the condition, that cannot
improve by changing your pattern of thought!"

Candace has thirty-five years in the fields of fitness, nutrition,
and natural health. As a coach in helping people with their *life choices*.
Candace offers a wide variety of tools to assist clients get in touch
with their "power" and find balance in their lives. She is a certified
trainer for mental health first aid classes.

She has been presenting workshops, seminars, and intensive
training to aid individuals in improving self-knowledge as well as
helping educate those who desire to know more about healing the
body with natural healing remedies.

Candace holds a BS, MS, doctor of naturopathy, and PhD in
nutrition. She is board certified with the American Naturopathic
Association and is a member of the Association for Nutritional
Consultants. She is also an Order of St. Luke Healing minister.

Published books:

- *A Workbook for The Warrior Within: A Guide to Inner Power*
- *Tough/Nice: A Manager's Guide to Sustained High Performance*
- *How Much Fat Are You Carrying? The Ultimate Fat Loss
  Guide for People Who Are Sick of Diets*

Printed in the USA
CPSIA information can be obtained
at www.ICGtesting.com
LVHW100847250923
759090LV00046B/504